Rhyming

This book belongs to

_____

FS109013 • Rhyming Words

hat   hat

cat   cat

Color the pictures that rhyme with **cat** .

bat

house

mat

tree

rock  rock

sock  sock

Color the picture that rhymes with **sock** .

net

lock

ball

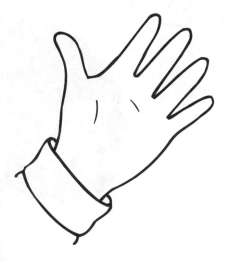

hand

FS109013 • Rhyming Words

bee

bee

tree

tree

6

FS109013 • Rhyming Words

Color the pictures that rhyme with **tree** .

hat

rock

three

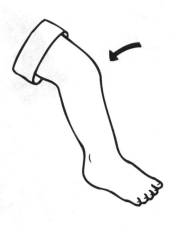

knee

bug

b̦u̦g̦

hug

h̦u̦g̦

FS109013 • Rhyming Words

Color the pictures that rhyme with **bug** .

mug

bird

flower

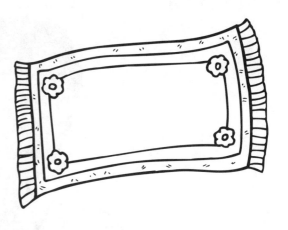

rug

can

can

man

man

Color the pictures that rhyme with **can** .

fan

pan

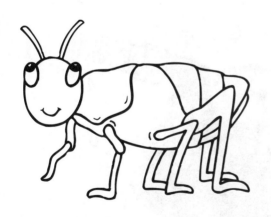

bug

fish

rose

hose

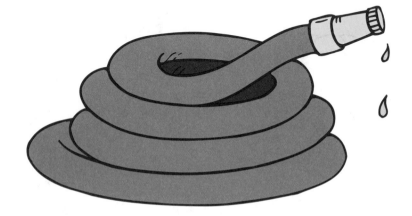

FS109013 • Rhyming Words

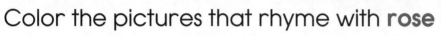

Color the pictures that rhyme with **rose** .

lips

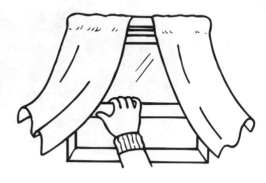

close

nose

pail

log

log

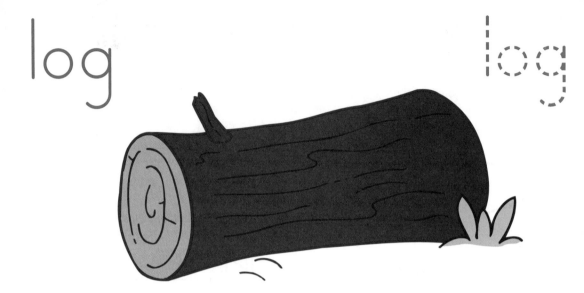

frog

frog

FS109013 • Rhyming Words

Color the pictures that rhyme with **frog** .

owl

dog

hog

cow

boat   boat

coat   coat

Color the pictures that rhyme with **boat** .

note

wagon

bear

goat

nail

nail

pail

pail

Color the pictures that rhyme with **pail** .

snail

fish

cat

mail

well

well

bell

bell

Color the pictures that rhyme with **bell** .

bucket

fell

shell

fish

gate

gate

plate

plate

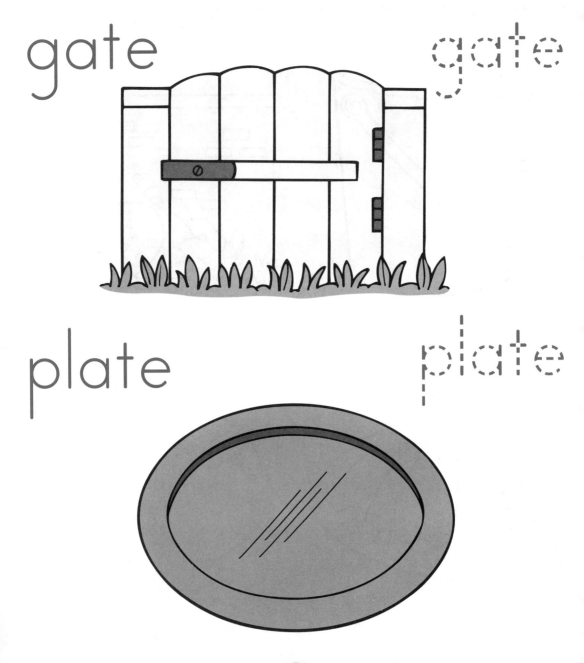

FS109013 • Rhyming Words

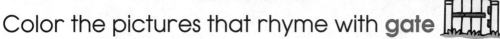

Color the pictures that rhyme with **gate** .

skate

ball

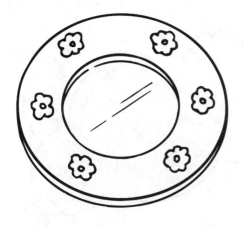

plate

bike

mop  mop

hop  hop

Color the pictures that rhyme with **mop** .

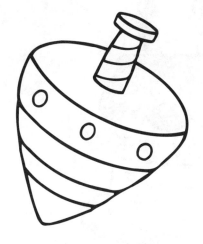

top

bus

doll

drop

cake

cake

rake

rake

FS109013 • Rhyming Words

Color the pictures that rhyme with **cake** .

hammer

lake

leaf

snake

Color the picture in each row that rhymes with the first picture.

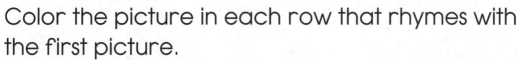
Color the picture in each row that rhymes with the first picture.

FS109013 • Rhyming Words

train

train

chain

chain

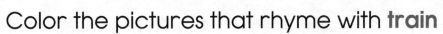
Color the pictures that rhyme with **train** .

apple   rain

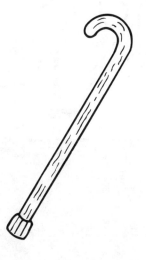

grapes   cane

hand

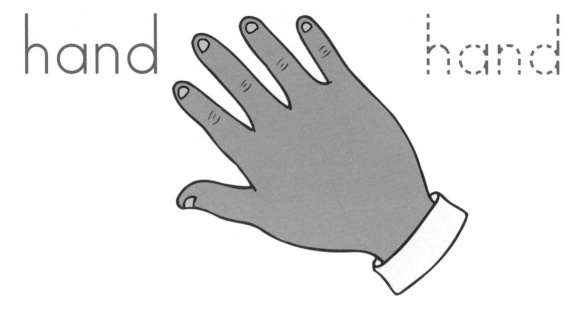

hand

land

land

FS109013 • Rhyming Words

Color the pictures that rhyme with **hand** .

sand

banana

mouse

band

hen

hen

pen

pen

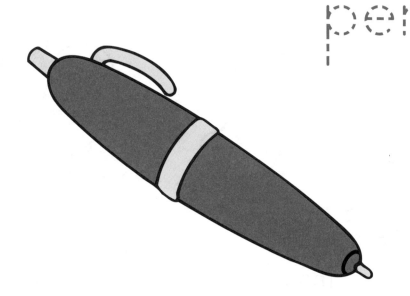

34

Color the pictures that rhyme with **hen** .

bear

boat

ten

men

ox

ox

fox

fox

FS109013 • Rhyming Words

Color the pictures that rhyme with *fox* .

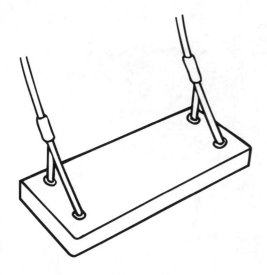

swing

box

socks

slide

pig

pig

dig

dig

Color the picture that rhymes with **pig** .

wig

ladybug

turtle

pail

king  king

wing  wing

Color the pictures that rhyme with **king** .

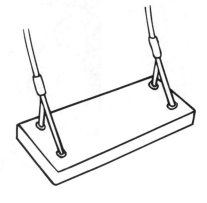

spoon

swing

ring

mug

bed

bed

red

red

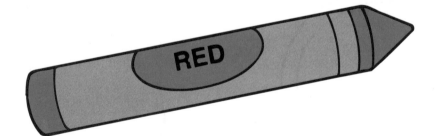

RED

42

Color the pictures that rhyme with **bed** .

red   dog

 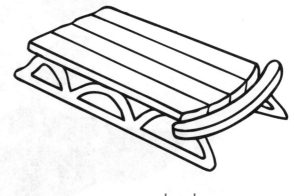

fox   sled

         FS109013 • Rhyming Words

shirt  shirt

dirt  dirt

Color the pictures that rhyme with **shirt**  .

skirt

shoes

socks

squirt

bag

bag

tag

tag

Color the pictures that rhyme with **bag** .

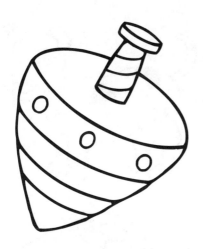

top

flag

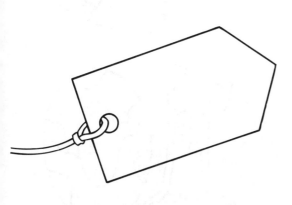

tag

horn

Color the pictures that rhyme with **boat** .

Draw lines to match rhyming pictures.

Color the pictures in each box ONLY if they rhyme.

Color the pictures that rhyme with **bee** .

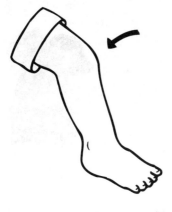

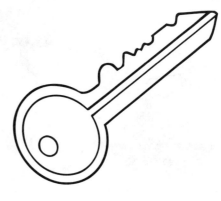

FS109013 • Rhyming Words

Draw a line from the **bug** to each rhyming picture.

Draw lines to match rhyming pictures.

Color the picture in each row that rhymes with the first picture.

Color the pictures in each box ONLY if they rhyme.

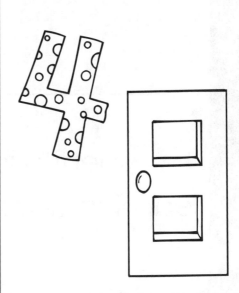

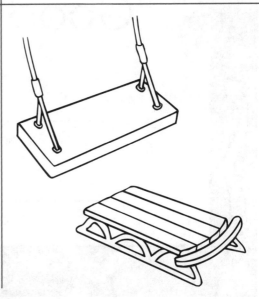

FS109013 • Rhyming Words

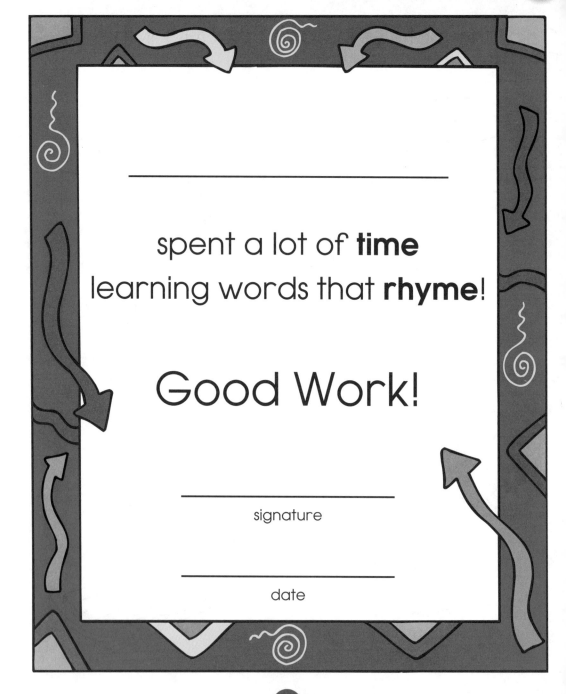

_____

spent a lot of **time**
learning words that **rhyme**!

Good Work!

_____
signature

_____
date